Getting Ahead *at Work*

Off to a Good Start | Learning the Job
Succeeding on the Job | Workplace Problems and Solutions

LIFE SKILLS

HANDBOOKS

Car and Driver

Community Resources and Safety

Consumer Spending

Everyday Household Tasks

Getting Ahead at Work

Health and Wellness

Managing Money

Moving Out on Your Own

Transportation

Workplace Readiness

SADDLEBACK
EDUCATIONAL PUBLISHING
www.sdlback.com

ISBN: 978-1-68021-985-2
eBook: 978-1-64598-783-3

Printed in Malaysia
26 25 24 23 22   1 2 3 4 5

TABLE OF CONTENTS

Off to a Good Start

Starting a new job is exciting. But it may also be scary. Doing good work is important. Getting along with coworkers matters too. You'll likely have many questions. Answers can often be found in the employee handbook. There are also things you'll figure out on your own in time. Learn faster by following some basic guidelines for starting a new job.

The First Two Weeks

Yasmin couldn't believe it. The past two weeks had gone by so fast. That's how long she'd been at her new job. She was working as an administrative assistant at a doctor's office. Overall, things were going pretty well.

Looking back, Yasmin thought about her first day. She'd filled out a lot of forms. These signed her up for health insurance and other benefits. Her manager also gave her a copy of the employee handbook. He told her to read through it. The handbook contained valuable information. Everything from paid time off to what employees were expected to wear was covered.

During the first week, Yasmin had met everyone in the office. She had been nervous. But her coworkers probably didn't notice. Yasmin had shaken their hands with confidence. Since then, she'd worked with several of them. Everyone was friendly and patient as they helped train her. They were happy to answer questions too. She really appreciated this.

Morgan and Lucy were two of Yasmin's new coworkers. At the end of her first week, they'd invited her to lunch. That really made Yasmin feel welcome. But the lunch had been awkward. Lucy shared many details about her personal life. Ever since, she'd been stopping by Yasmin's desk to chat. All this made Yasmin uncomfortable. She wasn't sure what to do.

Still, at the end of her second week, Yasmin had no worries. She was happy to receive her first paycheck. Yasmin looked forward to many more weeks at her new job.

Chapter 1

The Importance of First Impressions

Think about meeting someone for the first time. You get a quick idea of what the person is like. The opinion you develop is called a first impression. Usually, a first impression is formed within minutes of meeting someone.

When you start a new job, your coworkers will quickly form an opinion about you. What will they see? It's important to think about the image you present. Do what you can to make sure it's a good one.

Making a Good First Impression

1. **Wear clothing that's appropriate for the workplace.** It can be difficult to know what clothing is right for your workplace. Casual or informal clothes usually aren't a good idea. These make it seem like you don't care about your work. Wearing revealing clothes is never appropriate.

   What should you wear? A neat blouse or shirt and a nice pair of pants work well. Pay attention to what your coworkers wear. This will help you decide what is acceptable for your workplace. Also remember that in most cases, it's better to be dressed too formally than too casually. Don't be afraid to ask your supervisor about the dress code.

Tips for Making a Good First Impression

- **Don't be late.** On your first day, arrive a few minutes early. You don't want to keep anyone waiting.

- **Look presentable.** Your appearance is the first thing people notice. Make sure you're dressed nicely and are well-groomed.

- **Smile and have a positive attitude.** This will help put people you meet in a good mood.

- **Listen carefully and be polite.** Show interest in what others say. When you meet someone, use their name in the conversation. This will help you remember names.

- **Be yourself.** Don't try to impress people by being overly friendly or acting like you know more than you do. Have confidence in who you are.

2. **When you meet others in the workplace, be confident.** Look them in the eye and smile. Making eye contact suggests that you are self-assured and eager. Smiling shows you are friendly and pleased to meet someone.

3. **Concentrate on learning your job throughout the day.** Put all your effort toward doing things correctly. But don't worry if you don't do everything right at first. It takes a while to learn any job. Show that you are trying hard and willing to learn. Don't be shy about asking questions or seeking help. Your efforts will be noticed.

4. **Be on time.** Arrive at work a few minutes early. That way, you're ready to start on time. Go to lunch and take your breaks when you're supposed to. Don't take longer than you should or be late getting back. Both managers and coworkers will notice. These bad habits are easy to form. They're also hard to break.

5. **Don't expect or ask for special favors.** Remember that you're one of a group of employees. Your manager needs to be fair to everyone. Also, don't expect your coworkers to do your work or to cover for you. For instance, never ask a coworker to lie about your being late or leaving early.

Know the Dress Code

Most companies have a dress code. It tells employees what kinds of clothes they're expected to wear.

In many workplaces, the dress code is business casual. Business casual allows you to look professional but be comfortable. Don't take comfort too far, though. What you'd wear to a sporting event isn't usually appropriate for the workplace. Neither is what you'd wear when going out with friends. Also never wear clothing that's wrinkled, torn, or dirty. Remember, your appearance on the job says a lot about your attitude toward your work.

6. **Do work that you're proud of.** When it comes to your work, never settle for "good enough." Try to do a little bit better every day. Developing your work skills and abilities can be a real challenge. But over time, you'll discover the rewards that can come from doing well in the workplace.

Working Remotely

Some people today have the option of working remotely. This means they don't go into an office for work each day. Usually, they work from home. But they can often work from anywhere that has an internet connection.

When working remotely, coworkers interact online. They may use email, video calls, or an online chat program. If you are starting a new job and working from home, you might not get to meet your coworkers in person. But don't worry. You can still make a good impression when you meet them virtually. Here are a few tips:

- Test your computer equipment before your first video call. Check that your internet connection is strong and fast so you don't cut out. Become familiar with how to use the video call program. Learn how to turn on your video, share your screen, and mute your microphone. Also make sure you have decent lighting and that your computer camera is in a good position.

- Work when you're supposed to. Stay focused on work throughout the day. Working from home can present many distractions. Do your best to separate your work life from your home life. Treat your remote job like you would any other job. Don't handle personal matters on work time.

- Communicate with your manager and your coworkers. Working remotely means you'll be communicating with people differently than normal. It might not happen as naturally as it would in a regular office setting. Make an effort to speak with your new coworkers. Also speak regularly with your manager. Don't be afraid to ask questions.

- Set up a designated office space. Just like in a regular office, keep your work area tidy. Remove distractions. Try to find a quiet place where you can focus.

Chapter 2

The Employee Handbook

When you start a new job, your supervisor may give you a copy of the employee handbook. If you don't receive a handbook, ask if one is available. It may also be called the employee manual. Sometimes it will be available online.

Basic Information

The employee handbook contains basic information about your job and your workplace. This includes company policies. Shift times, sick leave, and paid time off are usually covered. Things such as the dress code and harassment policies are too. If you have a question about a work policy, check the handbook before asking your manager. Employee handbooks are designed to answer questions employees might ask. These may include:

- How do I report extra hours I've worked so I'll get paid the right amount?

- What should I do if I have an appointment during work hours that cannot be rescheduled?

- Where can I get a parking permit for the company lot?

- What holidays are covered as paid time off?

What's So Important About an Employee Handbook?

Having an employee handbook protects both the employee and the employer. The handbook outlines important company policies. It is like a contract. Employees are told what their employer expects of them. They also learn what to expect of their employer. When expectations aren't met, everyone knows what will happen. This is because it's stated in the handbook. In this way, an employee handbook helps create a fair and consistent working environment. Conflicts can be avoided. Unnecessary lawsuits are also prevented.

Employee Evaluations

The employee handbook may also explain how and when employee evaluations are done. These are sometimes called performance reviews. During your evaluation, your supervisor will give you his or her opinion about your work. You might also be shown a form that gives ratings or grades about specific things you do in your job.

Safety Information

Safety in the workplace is very important. An employee handbook may explain safety measures you should take. It will also likely explain what to do if you're injured on the job. For example, some people work with chemicals. Their company's handbook will likely say where to get help and how to call for emergency care if they've been exposed to a dangerous substance. The handbook may also note where first aid supplies can be found or how to help injured coworkers.

Complaints and Concerns

The employee handbook may also contain information on filing a grievance. A grievance is a formal statement of complaint or concern. Most workplaces have specific procedures for filing one. Following these steps will help your employer respond to your issue.

Grievances are sometimes filed in cases of harassment. Being repeatedly bothered or annoyed by someone else is considered harassment. At work, this may be another employee who keeps asking you to go on a date. It might also be someone who's touching you or hanging around you all the time. Having someone interfere with your work so you won't get credit for it is also considered harassment.

In any case, you shouldn't feel helpless. If you decide to file a grievance, someone will look into the problem. Then they will help with resolving the issue.

Dealing With Harassment

If you're being harassed on the job, keep track of what happens. You'll need these details to file a grievance. They'll also help to prove your case against whoever is harassing you. Follow these tips:

- Carry a notebook, and write down every harassing act, large or small.

- Record as many details as possible. This includes specific dates and times. Also write down everything that was said and done.

- Write down the names of everyone involved. Include the names of people who might have witnessed the harassment.

- Make copies of all your notes. Keep them in a safe place.

- Save recordings, such as harassing voice mails. Also keep any photos, emails, or text messages related to your claim.

Don't wait to report harassment. Find out how your company handles it. Then make a plan. There are rules about how long you have to report an incident.

Understand the Handbook

Be sure to read the whole handbook as soon as possible. If you don't understand something, ask about it. Your manager or someone in the human resources (HR) department should be able to help. Get everything clear in your mind early in your employment. Knowing this information will help you stay both satisfied and safe on the job.

Some companies have new employees sign a form saying they received a copy of the handbook. Then employees can't say later that they didn't know about workplace policies and procedures. This is another reason you should read the whole handbook.

Chapter 3

Fitting In With Coworkers

Job satisfaction stems from many things. One is your relationships with coworkers. Not all of these relationships will be the same. You'll really like some of your coworkers. They may even become your friends outside of work. But you may not get along as well with other coworkers. Interacting with them might be a challenge.

When you're at work, your first priority is to do your job as well as you can. That means you should try to get along with everyone.

Be a Good Coworker

When you first meet your coworkers, focus on remembering their names. Also pay attention to who does what. Learn people's job titles. Find out what they're responsible for. As you go about your job, notice how your coworkers do their jobs too.

Don't "borrow" supplies from coworkers. Even if you're in a rush, be sure to ask first. Never just take something—such as a pair of scissors or a pen—that someone else will need. This could annoy or inconvenience your coworker. Find out where supplies are kept. Then keep your own desk well stocked.

Finally, stay in your own work area. If you're always "visiting" someone else's workspace, then neither of you is working. Annoying your coworkers could get you in trouble. They may react by avoiding you or complaining about you.

Know What Not to Talk About

Avoid talking about your personal life while at work. Also steer clear of topics that might annoy or offend people. Keep your personal opinions to yourself.

Be aware of gossip. This exists at every company. It may be tempting, but try not to get involved. For example, you may want to agree with a complaint you hear about the company's vacation policy. You might also be curious about a coworker's personal life. Don't take part in such conversations. If you do, some people might think you're taking sides or spreading negative information.

Topics to Avoid in the Workplace

Some topics are considered inappropriate when talking with coworkers. Choosing the wrong topic can affect how people think of you in the workplace. It may also affect how they treat you. Here's a list of topics to avoid:

- family and marriage issues
- health problems
- financial troubles
- religion
- politics
- salary or wages
- career goals
- complaints about work

Tips for Avoiding Gossip at Work

- Don't share personal information about yourself or others.
- Stay away from the people and places involved in gossip.
- Change the subject when the conversation turns to gossip.
- Don't pass on the gossip you hear.
- Ask people who gossip to stop.

Facts About Office Gossip

A 2019 study of 529 office employees revealed some interesting facts about gossip in the workplace:

- The average employee spends 40 minutes per week gossiping with coworkers. That's almost 33 hours a year.
- 55% of male employees and 79% of female employees admit to gossiping.
- 29% of employees say that gossip is their main source of information about their workplace.
- Younger employees are more likely to gossip at work than older employees.
- In North America, nearly 75% of office workers admitted to gossiping in the workplace.

Create a Good Work Experience

When you're at work, stay focused. Do what you were hired to do. Think about what you want to accomplish. Set daily goals. Challenge yourself to do a little more each day. But keep in mind what your priorities should be. What does your supervisor want you to do first, second, and so on?

Be friendly toward your coworkers. Look for opportunities to help out when you can. Know that good manners count. It's never a mistake to be considerate or to thank someone who's helped you.

Show up with a good attitude each day. Remember, your work experience will only be as positive as you make it.

Today's Tasks:
- *Finish presentation*
- *10 a.m. meeting*
- *File invoices*
- *Schedule call with Jay*

Chapter 4

Interpreting a Paycheck

Receiving your first paycheck is a thrill. Getting paid makes all of your hard work feel worthwhile.

Many employers offer direct deposit of your earnings. That means an employer will put the money directly into your bank account. You don't have to take your check to the bank to deposit it. Some companies require direct deposit. But others let you choose. If you want to receive a paper check, you may be able to.

The Earnings Statement

No matter how you are paid, you'll receive an earnings statement, or pay stub. It's attached to your check or available to you digitally. Your wages or salary will be listed on the earnings statement. This is called gross pay. In financial terms, *gross* means "total" or "overall."

The amount you actually receive is less than your gross pay. That's because deductions are withheld from your earnings. Deductions are amounts of money taken out of your earnings to pay for other things. They may also be called withholdings.

After all the deductions have been made, the amount that's left is called your net pay. In financial terms, *net* means "remaining." Net pay is sometimes called take-home pay.

Deductions

Two deductions from your gross pay are required by the U.S. government:

1. **Federal income tax:** This is money you pay to help fund the U.S. government. It is a percentage of what you earn.

2. **FICA (Federal Insurance Contributions Act):** This is money you contribute toward Social Security and Medicare. These are funds that support senior citizens, people with disabilities, and others in need.

Federal Income Tax

Federal income tax is a percentage of your annual earnings. The rate is based on a person's income level. It's also different for people who are single, married, or have dependents, such as children. In 2020, a single person with no children paid these federal income tax rates:

Earnings	Rate
Up to $9,875	10%
$9,876 to $40,125	12%
$40,126 to $85,525	22%
$85,526 to $163,300	24%
$163,301 to $207,350	32%
$207,351 to $518,400	35%
Over $518,400	37%

You'll probably see other deductions on your earnings statement too. These may include:

- **State income tax:** This money helps fund your state government. Not all states have an income tax, but most do.

- **Health and dental insurance:** This money goes into plans that help pay your doctor and dentist bills. Your employer may offer several plans at various price points.

- **FSA (Flexible Spending Account):** You can use money placed in this account to pay eligible medical expenses. The money is not taxed.

- **HSA (Health Savings Account):** This is another type of account you can put money into for medical expenses. To set up an HSA, you must have a health insurance plan with a high deductible.

- **Disability insurance:** This money goes into a plan that pays employees who can't work because of injury or illness. If you got seriously hurt or sick, you would still get paid.

- **Life insurance:** You can withhold money from your paycheck for life insurance. In the event of your death, your loved ones will receive money to help them pay for expenses.

- **Retirement plans:** You can put a percentage of your earnings into a retirement plan such as a 401(k) or IRA account.

- **Charitable donations:** Some people have money withheld for donations to charities.

- **Union dues:** Workers who belong to a union can choose to have their union dues deducted.

Sample Earnings Statement

Every company has its own list of deductions. Here is an example. Rick Marshall works for the Applegate Cannery. His earnings statement is shown below.

APPLEGATE CANNERY   #5015

Earnings Statement   Rick Marshall
Pay Period: March 1–15, 2021

Employee Earnings
Gross Pay $895.00

Deductions

Federal Income Tax	$98.45
FICA	$71.40
Health Insurance	$107.40
United Way	$3.00
Union dues	$32.00

Net Pay   **$582.75**

Your earnings statement won't look exactly like Rick's. But you'll find some of the same categories of deductions listed.

Why should you know how to read your earnings statement? It's important for two reasons. First, you need to understand what all of the deductions are for. Second, you have to make sure each amount is correct.

When you begin a new job, speak with the person who handles payroll. Make sure all your information is correct. This will help you get paid correctly and on time.

Understanding Social Security

Social Security is a program that provides income to U.S. workers after they retire. You'll pay into the Social Security fund during your working years. When you reach the age of retirement, you'll be able to receive Social Security payments. Retirement age is between 65 and 67, depending on when you were born. Payments can also be started early, at age 62. However, the amount you receive will be reduced. Waiting to receive Social Security payments until later in life is also an option. Then the amount you receive will be higher.

Your monthly Social Security payments will depend on how much money you earn in your lifetime. The Social Security Administration (SSA) uses a special formula to figure this out. It's based on the 35 years in which you earned the most money. Keep track of this amount by checking your yearly statement which can be accessed at the SSA website.

Learning the Job

Starting a new job involves learning new skills. You'll also apply skills you already have in new ways. For instance, most jobs demand good communication skills. They also require working with other people. This includes managers and coworkers. Get off to a good start at your new job by learning how to apply some key skills.

Learning to Do Things Right

Jackson waited nervously at his desk. Karen, his supervisor, was in a meeting. She'd be getting out shortly. *Will she be upset with me?* Jackson wondered.

Two hours earlier, Karen had given Jackson a task. He was supposed to update some employee records on the computer. Later that week, Karen was going to have performance reviews with these employees. But she wanted their records updated today. That would give her time to review the information.

Karen had told him what to do. He'd even taken notes. But Jackson soon realized that he still had questions. Where exactly were the employee records stored on the computer? Who was supposed to check his work and sign off on the updated records? Jackson had only worked at the company for a month. This was the first time he'd done this kind of task. He struggled to remember everything Karen had said.

When Karen got out of her meeting, Jackson planned to ask her to repeat the directions. He would also ask questions about anything he wasn't clear on. That way, he'd understand exactly what needed to be done.

As it turned out, Karen wasn't upset with Jackson. She was glad he'd asked for help. Delaying the work for a few hours was much better than having it done incorrectly, she told him.

Chapter 1

Impressing Your Manager

Once you've gotten a job, there are new challenges to face. Impressing your manager is key. But what can you do to get recognized? What will keep you from being fired? How can you qualify for a promotion or raise?

Get to Know Your Company

Pay attention to news about your company. For instance, maybe your company is doing well and plans to hire more people. Perhaps it's involved in community events. Watch for stories in the local newspaper and on the local TV news. Also look for information on the company's website and social media accounts. Being interested in the company will show that you take your job there seriously.

Depending on what job you have or the size of your company, you may never meet your company's leaders. But it's still a good idea to know the names of key people. These include the company president and department heads. Knowing who they are will help you feel better connected to your company and its mission and values.

Before You Start

Prepare to impress your manager even before your first day at work. Learn everything you can about the company. If possible, talk to other people who work there. Also do some research online. Look for answers to questions such as these:

- How many employees does the company have?

- Does it have offices, warehouses, or sales groups in other locations?

- Who uses the company's services or products and why?

- How long has the company been in business?

Make an effort to learn about the company. Try to be as informed as possible. It shows you're taking your job seriously. Plus, knowing more about the company will help you in your daily tasks. Your manager is sure to notice.

On the Job

How can you prove that you're trying your best to be a good worker? There are many ways. Here are a few:

1. **Pay attention.** Learn how the best workers do their jobs. Take notes during meetings. Ask questions about company goals, products, and services. Show an interest in how your work fits into the company's plans.

2. **Be prepared for meetings.** Arrive on time. Bring paper and a pen to take notes. Also bring along any materials that may help with the discussion.

Guidelines for Good Meetings

1. **Take meetings seriously.** Show up on time. Pay attention. Don't leave early.

2. **Be prepared.** Bring along the agenda, or plan, for the meeting. Also bring a pen and notebook.

3. **Stay on topic.** Don't have side conversations. Also avoid discussing work topics that not everyone needs to know about.

4. **Be honest.** Take the opportunity to state your opinion or to share what you know.

5. **Follow through.** After the meeting, do what you're supposed to do.

3. **Volunteer.** Your supervisor may sometimes ask for help on a special project. By all means, volunteer. Doing so is a great way to show your enthusiasm and gain more experience.

4. **Do good work.** Try your very best to turn out a good product or service. Be agreeable when asked to do something extra. Speak up if you're asked for your opinion. Make suggestions and share ideas you have for improvements. No one will know what you can do if you never share what you think and know.

5. **Be patient.** Understand that it takes time to get recognized for your good work. But be confident that it will happen.

Much of what we communicate to others comes from our actions, not our words. Be sure to communicate confidence in the way you carry yourself. Here are a few ways to do so:

- **Make eye contact:** Looking people in the eye shows that you're comfortable talking to them. It lets people know you're interested and paying attention. Eye contact also shows that you're open and honest. Not looking people in the eye indicates all the opposites. People may think you're uneasy, not interested, not paying attention, and maybe even dishonest.

- **Smile:** Smiling in a natural way shows warmth and friendliness. It can put others at ease. Not smiling indicates worry, fear, or unhappiness. An unnatural smile can show nervousness or dishonesty.

- **Nod your head:** When listening to other people talk, nod your head slightly. This shows that you're focused and interested in what's being said. It also indicates that you understand and support what's being said. Frowning suggests that you disagree or don't understand.

- **Have good posture:** Standing or sitting up straight shows that you are secure in your surroundings. It also shows that you're paying attention and ready to participate. Slouching indicates that you're distracted and unsure of yourself.

- **Use your hands when you speak:** Making natural gestures while speaking shows energy and confidence. Not knowing what to do with your hands makes you seem uncomfortable or shy. Wild or jerky gestures indicate that you're nervous.

Chapter 2
Following Verbal Directions

Tomás is a new employee in a warehouse. So far, he's spent most of his time stacking crates with a forklift. But this morning, Tomás's supervisor, Mark, gave him a specific job to do.

"We need to make room for a new TV shipment," Mark told Tomás. "Move all the TVs we currently have here in Building A. Use the forklift to take them to Building C. Then stack them on the top level."

"We've got TVs in Building B too," Tomás said. "Do you want me to move them to Building C?"

"No," Mark replied. "Just move the TVs here in A."

"Then I'll need to enter them in the inventory for Building C, right?" Tomás asked.

"Correct," Mark said.

"Okay." Tomás nodded. "Would you like me to start right away?"

"Yes, please," Mark said. "As soon as you can. Thank you."

Understanding Verbal Directions

Mark gave Tomás verbal directions. When someone gives you directions that way, it's important to pay close attention. Spoken directions can easily be misunderstood.

How can you make sure you understand what you're being told? Listen for the *what*, *how*, and *when*. In the example about Tomás, these are the key questions to answer:

- *What* exactly does his supervisor want him to do?

- *How* should he do it?

- *When* does his supervisor expect him to start?

Asking for Clarification

If you don't understand verbal directions, ask questions right away. Asking for clarification shows that you want to do the job correctly. Most managers are willing to repeat the directions or explain them more clearly. Your ability to do the work well accomplishes their goals as well as yours. It also saves time for everyone.

Tomás wasn't sure which TVs to move, so he asked Mark for clarification. He also asked if he should start that task immediately. Asking these questions set him up for success.

Use Learning Tools

When verbal directions are too brief or too complicated, it's best to write them down. That way, you'll have something written to refer to. It might also help you to make a drawing to remember information. Think of other tools you can use to help you understand verbal directions.

Tomás made a simple map to help him remember Mark's directions. The map showed Buildings A, B, and C. Tomás added lines to show the trips he'd make in moving the TVs. Having a map built Tomás's confidence. He knew he wouldn't get mixed up.

After reviewing the map for a few minutes, Tomás started moving the TVs. He finished the job so quickly that Mark had him help coworkers with some of their assigned tasks.

What's Your Learning Style?

Everyone learns in different ways. These are called learning styles. There are three general styles. Which one sounds most like you?

1. **Visual learners like to see information.** They learn well by reading and taking notes. Usually, they prefer a quiet workplace.

2. **Auditory learners like to hear information.** They learn well by having things explained to them. Often, they will hum or talk to themselves. Background noise usually doesn't bother them.

3. **Kinesthetic learners like to learn by doing.** They enjoy putting things together and handling materials. These learners also like to move around. Some may have trouble sitting still.

Memorization Tricks

You may be expected to remember a series of steps or other key details as part of your job. You can use memorization tricks to help you remember important information. These tricks are called mnemonics. There are several different types:

- **Music:** Just like certain songs get stuck in your head, putting key information into a song can help you remember it. Easy to remember jingles work best. An example is how young children learn the letters of the alphabet by singing the ABC song.

- **Name:** These work by taking the first letter of each item you want to remember. The letters are then used to make a name. An example is ROY G. BIV which is used to help people remember the colors in a rainbow (red, orange, yellow, green, blue, indigo, violet).

- **Expression:** These also work by using the first letter of each item you want to remember. For an expression mnemonic, however, those letters are then used as the first letters in a series of words that is easy to remember. An example is using the phrase "Please Excuse My Dear Aunt Sally" to remember the order of operations in math: parentheses, exponents, multiplication, division, addition, subtraction.

Chapter 3

Reading Skills

Cooks read the orders that servers hand them. Delivery drivers read maps. Carpenters read blueprints. Railroad workers read lists of cars that make up a train.

No matter what you do for a living, good reading skills are essential. They'll help you understand how to do your job—and do it better.

Make Use of Instructions

Briona works as an administrative assistant. On her first day, she was asked to photocopy a 48-page report for an important meeting. The copy machine was complicated. She'd never used one like it before.

At first, Briona worried. She had no idea how to work the copy machine. Then she took a deep breath and pressed a button. Instructions lit up on the copier's screen. After reading them carefully, Briona followed the steps. By taking things one step at a time—and not panicking—Briona was able to do the job. The report was copied in time for the meeting.

Jason is an apprentice with Roy's HVAC. The company installs heating and cooling systems. One day, Jason was putting in an air conditioner. He'd helped his boss install this model once before. But today he was on his own—and he had a problem. Two important parts simply wouldn't fit together. Fortunately, Jason knew better than to force them.

Feeling desperate, Jason opened the instruction manual. By reading carefully, he discovered the problem. He needed a connector that was still in the packing crate. Once he located the missing part, Jason completed the job. This gave him great satisfaction. Next time, he'd know exactly how to do the whole installation.

Ty got a job as a customer service representative. All day long, he sat at a computer, wearing a headset and talking on the phone. After a few weeks, Ty's neck began to hurt. His manager gave him written guidelines about ergonomics. Ergonomics is the study of the safest, most comfortable ways for people to use equipment at work.

After reading the guidelines, Ty understood why his neck hurt. His computer monitor was too high. He decided to lower the screen. Within a few days, the pain in his neck had disappeared.

No matter what your job is, you'll need to solve a problem from time to time. Often, you'll be able to solve the problem easily if you know how to read and follow written instructions. These directions will guide you until you're sure of how to do something on your own. Try looking online for resources that can help you.

If you can't figure out how to solve a problem on your own, ask for help. Maybe one of your coworkers will know what to do. If not, go to your manager. Don't look at needing help as a sign of weakness. In fact, the opposite is true. It takes self-confidence to ask for and accept help.

Literacy in America

According to a 2014 study by the National Center for Educational Statistics, 43 million adults don't have basic reading skills. That's about 1 in 5 American adults. These individuals can't read an article in the newspaper or the directions on a bottle of medicine. They also struggle at work. Many stay in low-level jobs or lose jobs because they can't read.

Reading Directions

Understanding how directions are set up on a page will help you make sense of them. Look for these common features:

- **Titles and headings:** The title usually appears across the top of the page. Headings break up the page into main sections.

- **Lists:** Lists are used to split information into separate points or sentences. A numbered list usually means the information presents the steps or parts of something.

- **Bold type and capital letters:** Bold type and capital letters show that something is important.

- **Type size:** In general, big type is more important than small type. However, small type often includes important details.

- **Photos and diagrams:** These show what's being described by the text.

Chapter 4

Teamwork and Cooperation

Anyone who's ever played a sport knows about teamwork. It's the group effort that results in winning the game. Team members pull together. This helps them achieve their common goal.

Teamwork is part of most jobs too. Whether you work in an office or a factory, you'll likely be part of a team. Your team's success will require everyone to work well together. This is called cooperation.

Types of Team Members

Suppose your manager asks you to take part in a group planning session. What will you do?

Employees respond to requests like this in different ways. Some contribute a lot. Others sit and listen. They may say or do very little. Still others contribute nothing. These employees hope their coworkers will do all the work.

Being part of a team means being actively involved. How can you make a strong contribution, especially if you are a new employee?

Making a Strong Contribution

1. **Pay attention.** You need to thoroughly understand the project
    everyone is discussing. What does your manager expect the
    team to accomplish? Perhaps your team is planning a new
    product. This could be a new type of cookie at a small bakery.
    Maybe you're improving a service. At a bank, this could mean
    streamlining the loan application process. Your group may also
    be designing a long-term plan. An example would be adding
    more recreational classes at a community center. Whatever
    the team is doing, make sure you are clear about the project's
    goals.

2. **Be a good teammate.** At group meetings, express your
    willingness to cooperate. Contribute your ideas. But don't
    take over the discussion. Listen to others. Be open to their
    suggestions. Don't insist on doing things your own way.
    Compromise when it seems appropriate. You might even
    suggest combining your idea with someone else's to make a
    better plan.

3. **Know the deadlines.** As your team's plan goes into action, stay aware of any deadlines you have to meet. Mark them all in your calendar. Make sure everyone on the team knows these key dates. Also understand that not everyone will work at the same pace. If needed, be ready to help coworkers complete their tasks.

Remember that your team's goal is to successfully complete the project by the deadline. Each person's contribution should be valued for its role in the team's success. Show respect for your teammates' efforts. Compliment those who contribute extra time and energy.

What Makes a Successful Team?

1. **Communication:** Part of being on a team is communicating with your teammates. Share any new information you receive about a project. This helps keep everyone on the same page. Also be a good listener. It shows respect and helps a team to build trust.

2. **Efficiency:** Organize a project's workload based on each team member's abilities. This will keep a project moving along smoothly.

3. **Ideas:** Collaboration and sharing ideas with your team is key. Building trust and respect with your teammates can help foster creativity.

4. **Delegation:** Decide who will do what. Assign project tasks based on each group member's strengths and weaknesses.

5. **Support:** Remember that everyone on your team is working toward the same goal. Be willing to help if a teammate is struggling.

Guidelines for Teamwork

- If possible, don't have a single team leader. Share leadership or take turns.

- Encourage everyone to express opinions. Value what others say.

- Identify the strengths and skills of individual team members. Then assign responsibilities based on them.

- Meet on a regular basis and in the same place, if possible.

- Agree on how you will make decisions.

- Have clear expectations for what each individual will contribute.

- At difficult times, remind team members of their common goals and achievements.

Succeeding on the Job

Most workers are evaluated by their employers once a year. But why wait? You can evaluate yourself today. This will help you figure out how to improve your job performance. Set your own goals. Work hard to achieve them. Then you can succeed on the job. In doing that, you can put yourself in the position to get what every employee wants: a raise.

Planning Ahead

Ken worked full-time and took a class three mornings a week. That didn't leave him much free time. But he believed all his hard work would pay off.

His performance review was in two months. He hoped it would result in a promotion. An assistant store manager position was opening up. If Ken got the job, it would mean a raise. Ken would also get some benefits, including health insurance.

Ken had worked at Mario's Men's Store for almost a year. He'd started as a part-time sales associate working 25 hours a week. But after only a few months, the store manager, Kelly, asked if he'd be available full-time. She liked how he found things to do in the store when sales were slow. Several of his coworkers just stood around and talked when they weren't busy with customers.

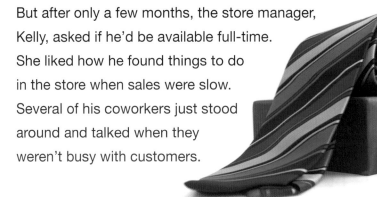

After Ken started working full-time, Kelly gave him more responsibilities. She also listened to his suggestions for how to display products. Together, they created a list of things for employees to do during slow periods.

Ken knew that the position of assistant manager involved recording each day's sales. He signed up for a class at the community college to learn basic accounting skills. Kelly thought this was a great idea. She agreed to change his hours at the store so he could take the class.

Kelly believed in Ken and wanted to support him. She wished all her employees were as ambitious as Ken.

Chapter 1

Measuring Your Progress

For six months, Hannah had been working as a hairstylist at a small salon. She could tell she was making progress.

For instance, Hannah had learned to be more efficient. By carefully scheduling her appointments, she was using her time well. She arranged her appointments in blocks of time. That way, she didn't spend hours each day waiting for her next appointment. When there was free time between appointments, Hannah took care of other tasks. These included ordering styling products and organizing her workstation. Not a minute of her time was wasted.

Having a set schedule also helped Hannah pick up more regular clients. People liked that she was available at certain times each day. Some set up appointments weeks in advance. Many of them also told their friends about Hannah. Then these people became her clients too.

Getting new clients meant that Hannah's income was steadily increasing. She was proud to be able to save part of her income. In a few years, she might be able to buy a townhouse. This excited her and made her work harder.

But Hannah's greatest satisfaction came from making her clients happy. She knew they were pleased with the way she did their hair. Some customers said they'd never felt better about the way they looked.

Evaluating Yourself

It's great to experience a sense of success on the job. Knowing that you're good at what you do builds confidence. But what if your job doesn't involve a growing list of clients? What if you're not seeing a steady increase in your paycheck? How do you know if you're making progress?

You can evaluate your own progress. Ask yourself these questions:

1. **Am I becoming an independent worker?** Being independent means you can do your work without constantly asking others for help. Once you become confident in what you're doing, you'll need less help.

2. **Do I catch and correct my own mistakes?** No one's perfect. That's why it's important to catch your own mistakes. You should also know how to correct them. If someone else is finding your mistakes, you need to put more effort into your work. Make sure it meets the expectations of your company. Don't ever take the attitude that someone else can fix it.

3. **Do I finish on time?** If you do good work within the time allowed for the job, then you're meeting the company's expectations. If you finish early and still do good work, then you're showing even greater competence.

4. **Do I have a growing sense of accomplishment?** If you feel that you're doing something worthwhile and take pride in your work, it will show. More importantly, your self-esteem will blossom. Having greater self-confidence will help you in any job you do.

Having Healthy Self-Esteem

Self-esteem is your overall opinion of yourself. It's based on how you feel about your abilities and successes. Your feelings about your limitations and failures play a role too.

People with healthy self-esteem value themselves. They believe other people should respect them and treat them well. Generally, they expect good things to happen.

Those with low self-esteem tend to feel that they're not good enough. Often, they worry about pleasing others. They don't expect to be treated well in return. In fact, these people usually expect bad things to happen.

Is it possible to have too high an opinion of yourself? Yes, and it's not healthy. Some people have an unrealistic idea of their skills and accomplishments. At some point, they will probably be very disappointed by a failure.

Learn From Your Mistakes

Everyone makes mistakes at work sometimes. Fortunately, you can learn from your errors. This will help you be a better employee. Ask these three questions to learn from your mistakes:

1. **Why did I make the mistake?** New employees usually make mistakes because they don't know how to do something. Employees who've been on the job for a while usually make mistakes because they're not paying attention.

2. **How can I correct the mistake?** If you know how to correct your mistake, then do it. If you don't know or need help, then ask for assistance.

3. **What else can I learn?** Mistakes create opportunities to learn more about your job. They also give you a chance to talk with your supervisor and coworkers.

Chapter 2

Efficiency: Speed and Accuracy

It's important to do your work correctly. But you also need to get it done on time.

Achieving one goal without the other won't help you succeed. If you make mistakes by going too fast, your output won't be satisfactory. Going too slowly may stop you from making errors, but your work will be late. Your goal should be to do accurate work that's finished on time. This is called efficiency.

Developing Better Keyboarding Skills

Tanya worked as a clerk in a used bookstore. Her job was to keep track of the books the store bought. Each book's title, author, publisher, and date of publication had to be entered into the computer. Its purchase date and price were entered too. Every entry had to be correct. The store used the list to sell books online.

Typing in the information accurately was easy for Tanya. But she worked much more slowly than the other two clerks. Tanya's supervisor showed her some typing exercises to practice on the keyboard. Within a week, Tanya could type faster and still make accurate entries.

"Remember," her supervisor said. "Practice makes perfect."

Learning Basic Office Skills

Many community colleges offer programs for training in basic office skills. You may even be able to earn a certificate to show you've completed a program. Office skills training is intended for people who want entry-level jobs in offices. Those jobs include receptionist, administrative assistant, and general office clerk. Programs often include courses in technology and communication skills.

Developing Better Carpentry Skills

Mike wanted to learn carpentry. He decided to become a carpenter's apprentice. This would give him on-the-job training.

The contractor who hired him needed help building a house. Mike was assigned to work under the supervision of a more experienced carpenter. His name was Kent. Together, Mike and Kent had to cut long boards into beams. These beams would hold up the roof. They were needed right away.

Mike quickly marked a board to cut. But in his hurry, he didn't place his tape measure on the board correctly. Kent stopped him.

"That will be too short," Kent said. "Measure it again. We need it now. But you'll waste material if you don't take the time to do it right."

"Sorry," Mike replied. He measured the board again.

"There is an old saying," Kent added. "It is 'measure twice, cut once.' That way you can be sure you measured correctly. If you measure once and cut the wrong length, you don't get a second chance."

Learning Basic Carpentry Skills

You can learn basic carpentry skills in several ways:

- **Watch educational videos.** You can find many of these for free online. Then practice what you've learned.

- **Read books and watch TV programs about carpentry and remodeling.** Again, follow up with practice.

- **Offer to help with a building project at the home of a friend or family member.** Pay attention to what the most skilled workers are doing.

- **Volunteer for a program such as Habitat for Humanity.** Learn basic carpentry skills while you help build homes for people in need.

Meeting Your Own Benchmarks

In addition to speed and accuracy, your job will have its own benchmarks. Whatever they are, strive to meet those standards. This will help you stand out as an exemplary employee.

But what if you don't meet those standards? What should you do? First of all, get some help. Ask your manager to work with you to develop your skills. Also ask for suggestions regarding courses or training programs you can take. Then, put in the time and effort needed to improve.

Second, don't give up. Learn from your mistakes, and then move on. Continue to strive to do your best. You'll get there.

Chapter 3

The Value of Soft Skills

Imagine you're a supervisor at French's Office Supply Store. You see that one of your employees, Sameer, does his job well and shows up on time. He's also pleasant to work with and doesn't fool around on the job. His creative-thinking and problem-solving skills are top-notch.

Sameer's soft skills really impress you. Soft skills are qualities and behaviors needed to succeed at work. Employers greatly value them. This is because they are more difficult to teach than technical job skills, such as how to use a computer. These hard skills can be learned. But without good soft skills, an employee won't do well on the job.

Next month is Sameer's annual review. As his supervisor, you'll need to give him feedback on his job performance. This includes hard skills as well as soft skills. You decide to spend some time evaluating Sameer on the job.

Top Ten Soft Skills That Employers Look For

1. growth mindset
2. creativity
3. focus mastery
4. innovation
5. communication
6. storytelling
7. cultural awareness
8. critical thinking
9. leadership
10. emotional intelligence

Solving Problems

You notice that Sameer always tries to solve problems that come up. He thinks about the store's goals when he's working. That helps him come up with good ideas. His ideas aren't complicated or difficult, but they work. Plus, they show that he's always thinking.

Here's an example: As Sameer's supervisor, you were disappointed in the sales of a hot new item. It was a laptop bag that had been on the shelf for a week. You thought it should have attracted more attention and sold better.

Sameer had an idea about how to sell more bags. He suggested moving them away from the computer supply area. Instead, a display could be placed up front. Most customers turned to their right when they entered the store, Sameer observed. Putting the bags there would draw more attention to them.

You decided to try Sameer's idea. At the end of the first day, French's had sold seven laptop bags. That was more than they'd sold the whole week before.

FRENCH'S
OFFICE SUPPLY

Job Security

Knowing that you aren't at risk of losing your job in the near future is called job security. This makes employees feel safe and less stressed, especially during uncertain times. You can increase your job security by:

- being a reliable employee.

- staying focused and avoiding distractions.

- helping out your coworkers.

- finding solutions to problems.

- offering to take on greater responsibilities.

- increasing your productivity.

- building strong relationships with your coworkers.

- participating actively in meetings.

- continuing to learn new, valuable skills.

Taking Initiative and Being Efficient

Sameer also took initiative. This means he handled tasks without being asked. One thing Sameer did was create new procedures for getting jobs done. In most cases, he found a more efficient way to accomplish the same task. When employees work better and faster, it saves the company money.

For instance, French's sale signs were being thrown in a box of jumbled materials in the storeroom. If someone needed a sign, it took a long time to find one. When a salesperson couldn't find a sign, sometimes he or she made a duplicate. That wasted both time and money.

Sameer set up a big file and put the signs in it. That allowed workers to find signs quickly. It also gave them the chance to spot worn-out signs and replace them when needed.

Teamwork and Communication

You also notice how Sameer interacts with his coworkers. Everyone seems to like Sameer. His positive attitude makes him easy to get along with. He is polite and considerate. People are always excited to work on a team project with him.

Sameer is a great communicator too. He listens carefully when others are speaking, especially when they're giving him instructions for a task. Afterward, Sameer asks questions to be sure he understands. When relaying information to other employees, Sameer is clear and concise.

As Sameer's supervisor, you know you can rely on him. His soft skills make him an excellent employee. At his annual review, you'll be giving Sameer a raise.

What Employees Value in a Workplace

- career development opportunities
- work-life balance
- great managers
- excellent compensation and benefits
- consideration for their personal health and well-being
- clearly defined job descriptions
- safe work environment
- desirable company culture

Chapter 4

A Strong Work Ethic

Has anyone ever mentioned your work ethic? Perhaps it came up during your annual review. Hopefully, your manager thought your work ethic was strong. But if not, don't worry. There are ways you can improve.

First, it's important to understand what work ethic means. This is a set of values. They serve as an inner guide to help you make good choices at work. Do you care about your job? Does this show in your actions? If so, you likely have a strong work ethic.

Showing You Care

Part of having a strong work ethic is showing that you care about your job. Take pride in your professional success. Value your work. Displaying the following skills will let your work ethic shine:

- **Dedication:** Be committed to your work. Stay focused. Have the discipline to follow through until tasks are complete. Learn new skills too. This will show that you're hardworking and want to improve at your job.

- **Integrity:** Build trust with your manager and coworkers by being honest and fair. Act in a consistent manner.

- **Reliability:** Be someone who others can count on. Show up on time. Do quality work in a timely manner. If you say you'll do something, get it done.

- **Productivity:** Work efficiently so that you can increase the amount of work you get done. Go above and beyond a project's basic requirements.

- **Professionalism:** Be aware of the image you portray to others. Dressing nicely and practicing good grooming habits show that you care. Always be polite and treat others with respect. Keep your workspace tidy.

- **Responsibility:** Hold yourself accountable for your actions. Own your mistakes. Find a way to fix the problem.

- **Cooperation:** Get along with your coworkers. Good teamwork skills are essential. Take on your fair share of a project, and do quality work. Offer assistance to coworkers who need help.

Setting SMART Goals

Part of having a good work ethic is setting and achieving goals. This will give you a sense of accomplishment. It's good to take pride in your work and achievements. Set yourself up for success by using the SMART goals method. These types of goals are:

- **Specific:** Make your goals clear and well defined. Answer *what*, *why*, *who*, *where*, and *how* questions.

- **Measurable:** Think in terms of *how many* and *how much*. A measurable goal lets you track your progress.

- **Achievable:** Set goals that are realistic. Don't make them impossible to reach.

- **Relevant:** Your goals should be meaningful to you. Set worthwhile goals that align with other goals that you and your company have.

- **Time-bound:** By setting deadlines, you'll be motivated to consistently work toward achieving your goals.

Develop Your Skills

Another way to show a strong work ethic is by improving your skills. Seek opportunities to learn and grow. You might attend conferences or watch webinars. Find out if classes related to your job are offered at a local college. They may also be available online. Read articles to stay up-to-date with happenings in your industry. Actively working to develop your skills shows that you care about your job. This will set you up for success in the workplace.

Tips for Developing a Good Work Ethic

- Have good time-management skills. Meet your deadlines. Show up to work and meetings on time.

- Be engaged during meetings and throughout the workday.

- Avoid distractions. Put away your phone and other devices while working.

- Keep your workspace organized. This includes your desk, computer, and paperwork.

- Set SMART goals. These will help you achieve more with focus and motivation.

- Take care of yourself. Avoid burnout with good work-life balance. Eating healthy foods, getting enough sleep, and exercising help too.

Workplace Problems and Solutions

People spend a lot of time at work. But not all of that time is pleasant. Sometimes, employees make mistakes. Then they likely receive feedback. Other times, coworkers have annoying habits. Some even bring their personal problems to work. Stay focused on your job by learning how to deal with common problems in the workplace.

Paying for Other People's Problems

"I need to get out of here!" Maddie thought to herself. She'd just come out of a customer service department meeting at work. Almost everything they'd talked about involved problems in the department.

Earlier that year, the company had laid off several customer service employees. Then the other employees had to take on more work. But because of her coworkers' bad habits, Maddie felt she'd taken on more work than anyone.

For instance, this morning, Tony was late again. It was the third day in a row. His being late meant that Maddie had to take his phone calls plus her own. To make things worse, Tony had asked her to lie about what time he'd come in.

Carla, another difficult coworker, was in the middle of a messy divorce. She talked about it all day long. Everyone in the department knew about her personal life. Some days, Carla spoke on the phone with her lawyer for 30 minutes at a time. Other days, she got so upset that she went home early. Maddie often took on Carla's work.

Maddie's worst coworker was Paul. He constantly made jokes about women. It wasn't unusual to hear him commenting on his female coworkers' clothing. His behavior offended Maddie. Sometimes she did his work just to avoid dealing with him.

Chapter 1

Be a Reliable Employee

Employers expect their employees to be reliable. Managers count on employees to do their work well and on time. Being punctual and staying engaged are also important. Your coworkers depend on you. Missing a deadline can throw off their schedule as well as your own. Take responsibility for your actions at work. Being a reliable employee helps keep everything running smoothly.

Becoming More Reliable

Your manager and coworkers need to know they can count on you in the workplace. But not all aspects of being a reliable employee may come easily to you. Luckily, there are ways to improve and become more reliable.

- **Manage your workload:** You might think taking on extra projects will make you look good at work. However, overloading yourself can have negative consequences. The quality of your work may suffer. Deadlines could also be missed. Only take on the amount of work that you can handle properly and complete on time. If you're feeling overwhelmed, speak with your manager.

- **Be punctual:** Being on time to work and meetings shows respect for your coworkers' time. It also shows that you care about your job. Aim to be early so that you have a few extra minutes in case something holds you up.

- **Communicate:** Sometimes circumstances are out of your control. If something comes up unexpectedly that will affect you getting your work done on time, speak with your manager right away. Make them aware of the situation, and come up with a plan to handle the issue. The sooner you mention a problem, the better. This gives you and your manager more time to work out a solution.

- **Own your mistakes:** Nobody is perfect. Everyone makes mistakes from time to time. The key is acknowledging your error. Address the problem as soon as you recognize it. Apologize and don't make excuses. Instead, focus on finding a solution. Make a plan so you don't make the same mistake again.

- **Surround yourself with reliable people:** Which of your coworkers are most reliable? Watch what they do at work. You may be able to learn from them. It also makes you look better if you associate with other reliable employees. Spending time with unreliable coworkers has the opposite effect.

Showing Up and Being on Time

Missing work can cause serious issues for an employer. Schedules are made based on employees being at work and completing tasks. All of us have days when we would rather sleep in, but part of being a responsible employee is showing up on time and being ready to work. Here are two common reasons employees frequently miss work:

1. **Burnout, stress, or low morale:** Some employees have a lot going on in their lives, and showing up for work is a challenge for them. Others may not feel engaged by their jobs, so they are not motivated to show up. But frequent absences cause problems for everyone. Employees should speak to their supervisor if they are having trouble getting to work regularly. They may need to evaluate whether the job is right for them. A supervisor might be able to help create a better work arrangement too.

2. **Poor health:** An employee who often misses work because of poor health needs to discuss the situation with his or her supervisor. Perhaps they can work together on a plan that will meet the requirements of the job. Maybe the employee's hours can be shortened or some of the work can be done at home. The supervisor may also suggest that the employee take a temporary leave of absence until his or her health improves.

Being late to work is also a problem. When an employee is often late, it's usually for one of the following reasons:

1. **Bad sleep habits:** If you frequently oversleep, get on a better sleep schedule. Try going to bed earlier. Then it will be easier to get up in the morning.

2. **Unreliable transportation:** Does your car often break down? An unreliable car might have to be replaced with a dependable bus schedule. Some people carpool to work. But what if the driver is often late? Try to find a ride with a coworker who is punctual.

Get Enough Sleep

How much sleep do you need? There is no "magic number" of hours. Every person is different. Age is one factor. Older people generally need less sleep than younger people. Quality matters too. If you wake up throughout the night, you aren't getting good sleep. Sleep debt also plays a role. This is  the total hours of sleep you've lost to being sick or staying up late. It adds up over time. Try getting more sleep to pay back your sleep debt. A nap after work could help you feel refreshed.

Most adults should try to get seven to eight hours of good sleep each night. But again, everyone's needs are different. Figure out how much sleep you need to feel your best. Then set a sleep schedule and stick with it. Wake up and go to bed at the same time every day. Turn down the lights and avoid electronics at least an hour before going to bed. This will help your body prepare to sleep.

3. **Poor planning:** Be sure to give yourself enough time to get ready for work. Figure out how long your morning routine takes. Also determine your commute time. Add a few extra minutes just to be safe. Set your morning alarm so that you have enough time to get ready without feeling rushed.

Others Depend on You

Showing up at work on time is only part of what it takes to be a reliable employee. Your manager and coworkers also depend on you to do your job. It's important that you work efficiently. This means doing your work well and completing tasks on time. Find a balance between doing your job quickly and without errors. Working too fast may mean mistakes slip through. But taking a long time on a task to make sure it's perfect is not good either. Missing deadlines can throw off everyone's schedule.

Being reliable also means you follow through. If you say you'll do something, do it. That includes handling the tasks you were hired to perform. Always do what is expected of you. This is an easy way to show your manager that you are a reliable employee.

Talk It Out

Sometimes things come up that prevent you from being on time or completing a task as instructed. No matter the situation, communication is key. Talk to your manager before they think you're completely unreliable. Don't wait for your manager to talk to you. By then, the issue will be harder to fix. Waiting will only make the problem worse.

Chapter 2

Receiving Negative Feedback

Connor McCormick is the shoe department manager at Swift's. This is a department store downtown. One day, Mr. Taylor, the store manager, calls Connor to his office. He tells Connor there have been some complaints about his department.

Two customers are unhappy. Both feel they have been ignored. One customer says she has tried to speak with Connor. But he hasn't seemed to care about improving the situation.

Think About What's Said

Mr. Taylor has never given Connor negative feedback before. Connor is shocked and embarrassed. Even so, he remains calm and listens.

Connor asks himself these questions:

- *Is the negative feedback valid?* In other words, is there a good reason the customers are upset?

- *Am I receiving constructive criticism?* This means that the feedback is intended to help an employee solve the problem.

Come Up With a Solution

Connor tells Mr. Taylor that he'll correct the situation. It will not happen again. He also thanks Mr. Taylor for bringing the problem to his attention.

That day, Connor starts working with his salespeople. They discuss ways to make sure customers feel satisfied. Together, they come up with several solutions.

Connor reports back to Mr. Taylor. He explains the new procedures he plans to put in place. Then he asks for Mr. Taylor's ideas about the new procedures. Finally, Connor thanks Mr. Taylor again for giving him the chance to solve the problem.

Dos and Don'ts for Handling Feedback

Connor handled the situation well. He remained calm and took time to think about the best thing to do.

What if Connor had not kept his cool? He could have:

- gotten angry.

- defended poor work.

- blamed his salespeople.

- criticized Mr. Taylor and pointed out his faults.

- changed the subject and tried to ignore the problem.

None of these responses would have been productive. Worse yet, any of them would have made Mr. Taylor think poorly of Connor.

Dealing with negative feedback is never easy. But think about it as a positive learning experience. Try to control whatever anger, hurt, or embarrassment you might feel. Then take time to think. Often, you can turn something bad into something good.

Tips for Handling Negative Feedback at Work

- **Listen carefully.** Many people shut down when they receive negative feedback. Instead, pay close attention to what is being said. You may even want to take notes.

- **Don't get emotional.** Focus on the facts, not on how they make you feel.

- **Wait to respond.** Don't interrupt. When your manager has finished speaking, calmly ask any questions that you have. Explain what you think went wrong. Be brief and sincere.

- **Don't hold a grudge against your manager.** Remember that giving feedback is part of their job. It is one way they help you become a better employee. Thank your manager for bringing the problem to your attention.

- **Decide how to correct the problem.** Consider what your manager said. Also think about what you know about the problem. Figure out a way to correct the problem, and then act on it.

What If You've Been Unfairly Criticized?

No matter how confident you are, you'll probably feel defensive after receiving negative feedback from your manager. Try to accept the criticism as valid and constructive. This will help you get over your defensive feelings. Be sure to take the time to think about the points made.

But what if you don't accept the feedback? You may feel that you've been unfairly criticized. If that is the case, follow these steps:

1. **When receiving negative feedback, stay calm.** Pay close attention. Take notes if you can. Above all, don't interrupt.

2. **Wait for your manager to finish talking.** Then say you'd like some time to think about their comments. Ask if you can meet again in a few days to talk about the problem and how to solve it.

3. **Afterward, go somewhere you can be alone.** Review your notes, if you took them. If you didn't take notes, write down the main points of the feedback. Do this right away, while you remember what was said.

4. **Plan for the follow-up meeting.** Write down questions you have about what your manager said. Also note any information they might not know or did not think about.

5. **When you meet, first thank your manager for agreeing to talk about the problem.** Then present your view. Speak calmly. Don't get angry.

6. **At the end of the meeting, accept your manager's decision— no matter what.** Say that you would like to solve the problem. Then follow through by doing what is expected.

Chapter 3

Bringing Personal Problems Into the Workplace

Having coworkers comes with many benefits. One is getting to know people and forming friendships. But those friendships should never interfere with doing your work.

Suppose your friend shows up at work very upset. She wants your help in solving a personal problem. What should you do? Offer to discuss it on your lunch break or after work.

You'll notice there are generally two kinds of employees in the workplace. Some are always bringing their personal problems to work. Others never do. Make up your mind to be one who doesn't.

For example, some coworkers go on and on about their hobbies, their children, or their dates. A few might complain about how little money they have. Other coworkers may continually discuss their health problems.

These behaviors prevent people from being reliable workers. Someone whose mind is busy with personal problems can't successfully do their job.

Try your best to leave personal problems at home. They don't belong at work. Your coworkers shouldn't have to be distracted by your life outside the workplace.

Imagine an invisible dividing line between your work life and your personal life. That should help keep the various parts of your life in a reasonable and workable balance.

Handling Conversations With Coworkers About Personal Problems

- Be positive and supportive. Don't take part in the complaining or criticizing.

- Stay logical and objective. Suggest alternative ways of looking at or solving the problem.

- Change the subject. Look for a way to naturally move to a different topic.

- Suggest meeting outside work to talk about the problem. Be clear about wanting to do work while at the workplace.

- Mention places to get help, if you can. Suggest joining a support group or going to a treatment center, if appropriate.

- Make your limits clear. If you're uncomfortable with the topic, don't hesitate to end a conversation.

Using Computers and Phones for Personal Business

Employees can cross the line between their work and personal lives in another way. This happens when they use their work computers to surf the internet. They might be shopping, making dinner reservations, or even looking for another job. Some employees also use their business email for personal communication with friends.

Other employees use the office phone for personal reasons. They talk at length about things that have nothing to do with work.

These behaviors take advantage of the employer. Any equipment, such as a computer or phone, that your employer provides is meant for work. The same is true for the time your employer pays you for.

It's okay to give your work phone number to your family. They should be able to reach you if there's an emergency. But it's not okay to use your company phone like it's your personal phone.

Making Personal Calls at Work

Make appointments and other personal calls during your breaks and mealtimes. Only make these calls from your work phone if absolutely necessary. It's better to make personal calls from your cell phone. That way, you will have some privacy. You also won't bother your coworkers.

Turn your cell phone to silent during the workday. Keep it in your desk, bag, or coat pocket. That way, you won't be tempted to constantly check it for calls, texts, and emails. If you're paying attention to your phone, you're not giving your full attention to your work.

Common Workplace Distractions

- smartphones and other devices
- noisy environments
- talkative coworkers
- constantly checking email and other messages
- social media
- long lunches/snack breaks
- the internet
- a messy workspace
- excessive/unproductive meetings
- multitasking
- management and policies that create unnecessary stress

Chapter 4

Relationships With Coworkers

When you enter the world of work, you'll meet many kinds of people. Some might be like the people you've grown up with. Others may have habits, manners, or speech patterns that are unfamiliar to you.

Some of your coworkers may dress or look different from you. They might have different values and beliefs than you do. Even the foods they bring for lunch may seem strange to you. You may not know how to act around them.

Accepting People's Differences

First of all, it's important to respect others' differences. It's easy to form opinions about people and things we don't understand. But differences don't have to be problems. Try to get to know people who are different from you. Keep your mind open. Be willing to learn from others. Hopefully, what you learn will make you less critical.

Once you begin to understand people, you'll respect them more. In fact, it's a good thing that everyone isn't the same. If we were all alike, we'd live and work in a very boring world.

Diversity in the Workplace

Many employers are providing diversity training for their employees. In the workplace, diversity involves all the characteristics that make employees unique. This includes race, ethnicity, gender, age, sexual orientation, religion, political views, and physical abilities. Having a diverse workforce means a company has, and can take advantage of, many different perspectives and ideas.

Diversity training helps coworkers understand how they are alike and different. It also helps them learn about and be accepting of each other. This can foster collaboration and creativity as well as create a more welcoming work environment for all employees.

Facing Discrimination

Another challenge may be dealing with discrimination. Discrimination can be displayed in several ways. For instance, a coworker who tells jokes that make fun of your religion is discriminating against you. A coworker who makes negative comments about your culture or language is too.

If you're in a situation like this, ask the coworker to stop the offensive behavior. If they don't stop, talk with your manager about the problem. You can also file a complaint about the coworker's inappropriate behavior.

Dealing With Difficult Personalities

Sometimes you may simply dislike a certain coworker because of their personality. In that case, just make it your goal to get along. Focus only on the work you do together. If you're polite, considerate, and focused on doing a good job, the other person will notice. You may even be surprised to find that your positive behavior has an influence on your coworker. That will make the situation much easier.

Fighting Discrimination in the Workplace

The Equal Employment Opportunity Commission (EEOC) is a U.S. government agency. It enforces laws that protect people from discrimination in the workplace. Discrimination can occur because of someone's race, religion, gender, sexual orientation, skin color, national origin, age, disability, or medical condition.

In the United States, it is illegal for an employer to discriminate against a job applicant or employee. Discriminating against someone who complains about discrimination and perhaps files a charge against an employer is also illegal.

An Inclusive Workplace

Many companies see the value in an inclusive work environment. This is when all employees can be their true selves while on the job. Background, circumstances, and identity do not matter. Differences are embraced. Everyone is made to feel welcome and included. In an inclusive workplace, all employees feel valued, have their voices heard, and are empowered to succeed.

Finally, try to be aware of coworkers' special situations. Someone may have experienced a death in the family or be going through a divorce. Perhaps another is dealing with a seriously ill family member. In these cases, do what you can to make things easier for the coworker. Don't neglect your own work. But try to be considerate with a coworker who's struggling.

Be a Good Coworker

Whether remotely or in person, coworkers spend a lot of time working closely with each other. It's not uncommon to get on each other's nerves from time to time. Follow these tips to ensure that you are a good coworker:

- Be on time to work and to meetings.
- Avoid eating smelly foods in the office.
- Have a positive attitude and don't complain.
- Maintain a neat workspace.
- Stay focused and on task.
- Try not to act like a know-it-all.
- Don't interrupt when others are speaking.
- Dress appropriately and practice good hygiene.
- Avoid being noisy.
- Be respectful and considerate of others.
- Don't sell products or solicit donations.

Enjoying Your Work

A new job can fill you with a mix of emotions. It's an exciting experience. But you may also feel nervous. That's normal too. Get to know your coworkers. Pay close attention when learning how to perform your job duties. Communicate with your manager often. Don't be afraid to ask questions. Stay focused while working. Go above and beyond. You'll soon find yourself on the path to becoming a star employee. If you enjoy your work, you may even turn your job into a career.

GLOSSARY

administrative assistant: a person who supports a company or department by handling tasks such as data entry, appointment scheduling, filing, and correspondence

ambitious: desiring fame, power, or success

apprentice: a person who is learning a skill or job from an expert

benchmark: a standard that can be used to judge the level or quality of other things

benefit: something given by an employer in addition to pay, such as time off

career: a job that someone does for a long period of time; often requires special training or education

clarification: the act of making something clearer and easier to understand

commute: the trip a person regularly makes from one place to another

competence: the ability to do something well

compromise: a way of coming to an agreement in which each side gives up something they want

concise: using few words or only necessary information

confidence: belief in oneself and one's abilities

constructive criticism: reasonable and fair feedback given to someone so that they can make improvements

contractor: someone who is hired to perform work within a certain amount of time for a certain price

contribute: to give something, such as time or money, to help a person or group

deductible: the amount of money someone must pay to fix something before their insurance company will begin to cover the rest of the cost

discrimination: unjust treatment of people based on their age, race, gender, sexuality, or beliefs

efficient: able to adequately complete a task without wasting time, energy, or materials

engaged: busy with an activity

evaluation: a careful and thoughtful assessment of someone's performance

exemplary: excellent and deserving of admiration

human resources (HR): a department of a company that deals with the company's employees

influence: the power to affect someone in an important way

installation: the process or act of preparing something for use in a certain place

interfere: to get involved in other people's activities and concerns in an unwanted way

lay off: to end a worker's employment, sometimes temporarily

leave of absence: a period of time when an employee has special permission not to work

payroll: a list of a company's employees and the amount of money each is paid

priority: something to which you give special attention

promotion: the act of moving an employee to a higher position within a company

punctual: doing something at the planned time

reliable: trusted to do what is needed

retirement: the period of time after someone permanently stops working

self-assured: acting in a way that shows belief in oneself and one's abilities

shift time: the hours that someone is scheduled to work

streamline: to make a process simpler and more efficient

union: a group of workers who join together to speak up for their rights

valid: reasonable or fair

wages: money paid from an employer to a worker on a regular basis

withhold: to hold something back, such as money

LIFE SKILLS HANDBOOKS

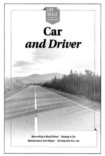

9781680219821

9781680219913

9781680219838

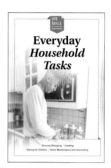

9781680219845

9781680219852

9781680219869

9781680219883

9781680219890

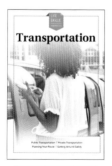

9781680219906

9781680219876

For more information, visit:
www.sdlback.com/life-skills-handbooks